Super Sleuth Inves...

in

Fruit Encounters
of the God Kind

BY

Christopher P. N. Maselli

Carson-Dellosa Christian Publishing
Greensboro, North Carolina

CREDITS

It is the mission of Carson-Dellosa Christian Publishing to create the highest-quality Scripture-based children's products that teach the Word of God, share His love and goodness, assist in faith development, and glorify His Son, Jesus Christ.

". . teach me your ways so I may know you. . ."
Exodus 33:13

For the mysterious Bongo Rod, aka Rod Butler, who loves classic mysteries.

Author ....Christopher P. N. Maselli
Editor ....Sabena Maiden
Layout Design ....Mark Conrad
Illustrator.................................Stefano Giorgi
Cover Design and Illustration.....Nick Greenwood

TABLE OF CONTENTS

CONFIDENTIAL INFORMATION

FOR YOUR EYES ONLY!

Greetings, Super Sleuth! You're about to embark on a series of great adventures as you solve mysteries with Nova and me, Mick. We're best friends and business partners with equal stakes in Super Sleuth Investigations, Inc. By "equal stakes," I mean we both came up with the idea of solving mysteries together for fun. And we're good at it. You can be, too!

This book is packed with 12 mind-bending mysteries that will challenge you to find clues and unravel the answers for yourself. The best part is, at the same time, you'll discover the mysteries of the Bible, too, because Nova and I believe God's Word holds the solutions to all of life's mysteries.

In this installment, we're going to dive right into the fruit of the Spirit. After a strong overview, we'll take a peek at love, joy, peace, patience, kindness, goodness, faithfulness, gentleness, and self-control. Then, we'll see how they all work together to help us live strong lives for God.

I'll be honest—living a life with the fruit of the Spirit alive in you isn't always popular, but it's necessary. It's the kind of life God wants us to lead—one that's consistent, upright, and very rewarding. It's the kind of life that will share the love of Jesus with the world!

GET "IN THE KNOW"

OK, so this book is important . . . but it's also fun because you can use it in so many ways! If you've never read one of our mystery books, allow me to show you how it works.

If you're a kid, you can buzz through this just like any other book, reading the mysteries one after another for a good time. Oh, wait! There's a neat twist: we don't come right out and tell you the solution to the mystery once we've solved it—we give you the chance to sleuth it yourself! Once you've gathered the clues and think you know the answer, you can read the solution box to see if you're right.

If you're a teacher or Sunday school instructor, you'll love the fact that each book contains 12 mysteries. So, if you do one a week, you'll have enough for a full quarter. You may decide to hand out copies of the mysteries and read them aloud with the class, so that students can look for clues as they go. If no one can solve the mystery, you can go over the story again, stressing key clues until everyone's on the same page. See page 48 for ways to create your own case files!

But the fun doesn't end there! After each mystery, there is a section called *Under Investigation*. This section is like a personal spy journal for writing down ways you can put the Biblical truth you discovered into practice. We've also included a *Word Inspector*, which provides a related Bible verse to memorize. And, at the end, you'll find a tough activity to crack. It's plenty of fun for everyone. So, get ready . . . and start sleuthing!

CHOP, CHOP!

"You do it!" Mick whispered.

"No, you do it!" Nova whispered back.

"We'll both do it," Mick finally said.

Mick shifted aside, and he and his best friend Nova rapped on Mr. Sapps' front door at the same time. As they waited, the two friends brushed off their sleeves and stood up straight, attempting to appear as professional as possible. They felt looking professional was important, because sometimes adults don't take twelve-year-olds seriously.

After a few moments, the door popped open. Mr. Sapps, a balding man with a thick mustache, stood there with a blank look on his face.

Mick put his hand forward. "Mick Gumshoe," he said, "from Super Sleuth Investigations. We're ready to solve your whodunit."

Mr. Sapps eyed Mick, then Nova. "You're the investigators?"

"The best you'll find on the supermarket bulletin board," Nova said confidently.

Mick nodded as he shook Mr. Sapps hand. "This is my partner, Nova Shrewd."

Nova smiled.

"You're kids," Mr. Sapps said.

Mick smiled. "We solve mysteries for fun. We won't charge you a cent."

Mr. Sapps shrugged. "The price is right. C'mere." The man walked between Mick and Nova and led them

to the center of his front yard. He held out his arms. "What's wrong with this picture?"

Mick and Nova looked around. They were surrounded with bright green trees of various heights. Many of them had large fruits hanging from their branches, such as peaches, oranges, and pears.

Mick pointed to a tree laying on the ground. "Why did you chop that one down?" he asked.

"I didn't," Mr. Sapps said. "But I want you to figure out who did. This happened last night while I was away."

Nova picked up an apple. "It was obviously someone who doesn't like apples. Do you have any clues?"

"That's why I hired you," Mr. Sapps said. "But I have some ideas. I've narrowed it down to one of my three neighbors. Ms. Smith has always complained about this apple tree blocking her view of the road. Mr. Davis doesn't like my trees in the autumn because the leaves fall and blow into his yard. And Mrs. Gordon says my fruit attracts squirrels and rodents. Any one of them would have had reason to chop down my apple tree."

Mick nodded. "Don't worry, Mr. Sapps. We'll find out whodunit."

As they walked down the street, Nova asked Mick, "How can you be so sure?"

"Because," Mick said, "we know all about fruit even if it's a different kind—the fruit of the Spirit."

"You mean love, joy, peace, patience, kindness, goodness, faithfulness, gentleness, and . . ."

"Self-control," Mick completed. "We have God's fruit active in our lives. It's the power of God working through us to do good. And to solve this mystery, we're gonna need that fruit!"

Nova and Mick arrived at Ms. Smith's doorstep. "You do it!" Mick whispered in a hushed voice.

"No, you do it!" Nova whispered back.

"We've really got to figure out who's going to knock," Mick said as he finally knocked on the door. A small, old woman with blue eyes answered.

"Hi," Mick said. "We're investigating a crime in the neighborhood. Someone chopped down Mr. Sapps' apple tree and—"

"—and you think I did it?" the old woman shouted. "Do I look like I could chop down a tree?"

Mick swallowed hard. Nova put a hand on his arm. "We're just searching for clues," she said. "Did you see anyone in his yard last night?"

"How could I?" Ms. Smith exclaimed. "His apple tree blocks my view!"

"But it was the apple tree that was cut down."

"Good."

"Good?"

"Good. I'm glad. I don't have to look at it anymore. But I cannot tell a lie. I didn't chop down the cherry tree."

"It was the apple tree," Mick corrected.

"I think that was a joke," Nova whispered.

The next stop was to see Mr. Davis. Mick and Nova caught him opening his door to get his newspaper. He was a large man with beady eyes and wispy, black hair.

"You talk to him!" Mick whispered in a hushed voice.

"No, you do it!" Nova whispered back.

"I can hear you," Mr. Davis said. "What do you guys want?"

"We're trying to solve a mystery," Mick said. "Someone chopped down Mr. Sapps' tree, and we're looking for clues as to who did it."

Mr. Davis shook his head. "I've never liked his trees—they drop leaves on my lawn—but I can't believe someone chopped one down. That's just not right. When did it happen?"

"Last night," Nova said. "Did you see anyone in his yard last night?"

Mr. Davis yawned. "I just woke up after a long night working. When I left for work last night, I thought I saw a woman over there. I can't be sure. But, I cannot tell a lie. I didn't chop down the cherry tree . . . or the apple tree for that matter."

Mick and Nova chuckled. Everyone was a comedian.

The last stop was to talk to Mrs. Gordon who was peeling out of her driveway when Mick and Nova arrived at her house.

"Wait!" Mick shouted, flagging her down. She stopped.

"Yes?"

"We're just wondering if—"

Mrs. Gordon's eyes shifted quickly from her backseat to the side view mirror. "I'm in a hurry," she stated, "spit it out."

"Did you see anyone in Mr. Sapps' yard last night?"

There was a long pause, then, "No . . . why?"

"Someone chopped down his apple tree," Nova said.

"I cannot tell a lie," she began.

Mick put up his hand. "Wait—don't say it."

"Please don't!" Nova said.

"Besides," said Mick, "it's really not necessary. I already know who did it."

"You do?" Nova questioned.

Mrs. Gordon quickly peeled away, not looking back.

"Of course!" Mick said, waving the road dust away. "This mystery was really quite easy."

Do you know who chopped down Mr. Sapps' apple tree?

How does Mick know? What was the clue?

Read the solution on page 8 to find out!

SOLUTION

"Easy?" Nova shouted. "I have no clue at all who did it!"

"Well, you should," Mick said. "We got a big one when we talked to Mr. Davis."

"You mean when he said he saw a woman in the yard last night?"

"No, that wasn't it. He was just trying to throw us off. Mr. Davis was the one who did it."

Nova blinked. "How do you know?"

"Because, he said he couldn't tell a lie. He didn't chop down the apple tree."

"So . . ."

"So, we never told him it was an apple tree. How would he know that if he'd worked all night and been asleep all day?"

"Yes!" Nova shouted. "Let's go tell Mr. Sapps that SSI has done it again!"

Under Investigation

Why do you think the fruit of the Spirit are called "fruit"?

Which fruit of the Spirit do you think is strongest in your life?

Which fruit of the Spirit do you think needs to get stronger?

What can do you this week to make that fruit stronger in your life?

But the fruit of the Spirit is love, joy, peace, patience, kindness, goodness, faithfulness, gentleness and self-control.

Galatians 5:22-23

Fruit Fit

Can you fit each fruit of the Spirit into the puzzle below?
Hint: If you can't remember all of them, look in the Word Inspector above!

THE TROUBLE WITH CANDY

"My little sister always listens in on my phone calls!" twelve-year-old Barb cried. "I love her, but she's driving me nuts!"

Mick turned to Nova and raised his eyebrows. Nova raised hers back.

"Well," Mick said, "I'm sorry to hear that, but what would you like us to do? We're private eyes, not parents."

"Ha-ha," Barb said, leading the investigators upstairs. "I hired you because I need you to grill her and find out how she's listening in."

Nova interjected, "I'm not sure I understand."

"I can't ever catch her in the act," Barb explained. "I'm sure she has a phone hidden in her room somewhere, but I don't know where."

At the doorway of Barb's little sister's room, Mick peeked in. Across the room, a young girl, about eight years old, played with a doll.

As Mick looked around, he saw that there were dolls everywhere. He pushed the door open slowly, noticing the nameplate on the door which read "Candy."

"Hi, Candy," Mick said. "My name is Mick, and this is Nova. Can we talk to you a moment?"

Candy's big brown eyes shifted from Mick to Nova, then to her sister. "OK," she said.

Mick entered the room, stepping over a few dolls on the floor. He picked up one and set it inside a big, blue doll house complete with white shutters and a welcome mat. "You have a lot of dolls," Mick said.

"I like dolls," Candy replied, placing one in a doll crib beside her bed. She removed a pacifier from its mouth, shoved in a toy bottle, and turned on a baby monitor. "Shh," she said, "Goober is going to sleep."

"Your baby's name is Goober?" Nova asked.

"All of her dolls have weird names," Barb said. She pointed to a doll across the room. "That one's Booboohead."

Mick nodded. "I like Booboohead. I once had a fish named Booboohead."

"Um, can we get on with the investigation?" Nova asked.

"Right," Mick said. "OK, so we're here to ask you a few questions, Candy. First of all, do you listen in on your sister's phone calls?"

Candy said, "Barb talks about boys all the time."

Barb huffed, "In other words, yes, she does. And I do not talk about boys all the time."

"Do, too. I know you like Carl Phinney because he has red hair."

"I do not!"

Mick asked, "Did you say

that on the phone?"

Barb hesitated. "OK, fine, yes. See, I told you she listened."

Nova asked Candy, "Do you have a phone in your room?"

"No," Candy said. "I don't need one."

Mick narrowed his eyes. "Do you follow your sister around and listen to her phone calls?"

"I can answer that," Barb said. "She doesn't. I've tried to catch her sneaking up on me, but she's always in her room."

Mick patted Goober on the back. "She's sleeping well." He looked over at Booboohead. "She seems very content, too." Then he looked at Candy. "You know Barb loves you, don't you? She told me that."

Candy nodded.

"Love is a strong thing," Mick said. "It's one of the fruit of the Spirit, and the Bible says it never fails. You can count on it to always come through. Now, we want to know if you love your sister enough to stop bugging her by listening to her phone calls."

Candy twisted her lip. "I guess so."

"Great," said Mick, "and the mystery is solved."

"Solved?" Barb cried. "How can you say it's solved? I still don't know how she does it!"

Mick grabbed a baby blanket and placed it on Goober's stomach. "That's an easy one," he said.

Do you know how Candy listens to the phone calls?

How does Mick know? What was the clue?

Read the solution to find out!

SOLUTION

"So, how does she listen to my calls?" Barb asked.

Mick looked at Nova, who smiled back. She walked over to the toy crib and pulled out the baby monitor.

Mick said, "I'm betting if you look in your room, you'll find the other monitor. That's how she hears your phone calls—at least your side of them—without actually using a phone."

Barb's mouth dropped open. Then, she broke into a smile. "Candy, you are such a stinker!"

Candy giggled. "Takes one to know one!"

"Case closed," Mick said happily.

Under Investigation

Is there someone you know who needs love?

What can you do this week to show that person God loves him?

Why do you think God wants us to show love to others?

Love never fails.
1 Corinthians 13:8

Word Inspector

Memory Quiz

Look closely at the picture below, then cover the picture and look at the upside down questions in the Memory Quiz box to see if you can answer them.

Memory Quiz

5. What time is on the clock?
4. What is sitting on top of the bookcase?
3. What does Candy have in her left hand?
2. Who is wearing sunglasses?
1. What number is on Mick's shirt?

THE CASE OF THE STOLEN JERSEY

"I didn't take it! I'm telling the truth!"

"Liar!" yelled Rock Johanson, one of the Shark's star soccer players. He had his teammate Sammy pressed against the wall.

Mick Gumshoe and Nova Shrewd stopped in their tracks when they saw the fight about to break out.

"Do something!" Nova whispered in a panicked voice.

"You do something!" Mick whispered back.

"We'll both do something," Nova finally said, stepping forward. She tapped Rock on the shoulder. He jumped.

"What?" Rock cried.

"Well," Nova started, "I don't think you want to beat him up."

"Why not?"

"Because . . ." Nova grabbed Mick's shirt and pulled him in front of her. "Tell him, Mick."

Mick stuttered. "Th-th-the thing is . . . if you beat Sammy up, that'll hurt your team, right? You all need to be healthy and strong if you're gonna beat the Tigers next week."

"We can do just fine without number 12," Rock said, peering at Sammy.

"No, you can't," Nova stated flatly. "You need everyone. Each player is necessary for a strong team."

Rock briefly tightened his grip on Sammy, then let go, obviously still upset. Sammy straightened his jersey and shook his head.

"I dunno what got into you, Rock. I didn't steal your shirt," Sammy said.

Rock bit his lip and turned to Mick and Nova. "He's lying," he said. "My jersey disappeared out of the locker room last week, and today I saw him wearing my jersey with my own two eyes."

"You're sure you saw him?" Nova questioned.

"Without a doubt. I was backing out of the school parking lot when I saw him give high fives to a bunch of our friends—and he was

CD-204035 *Fruit Encounters of the God Kind*

wearing my jersey!"

"I wasn't!" Sammy insisted.

"I saw you this morning—with Erin, Chip, and Katie, outside the library."

Sammy gulped. "I . . . I was there, but, Rock, I promise, I wasn't wearing your shirt—I didn't take it."

"Then, who did?" Rock demanded.

"How should I know?"

Rock huffed. "This is awful, this is awful," he said with frustration in his voice. "I know you did it."

"Can't you just wear a different jersey?" Mick asked.

Rock shook his head. "I only have one. People—my teammates—are expecting to see number 51 on the field. Besides, another number on my back could mess up our plays."

"I'll tell you what could mess you up worse," Nova said, "is if you lose your joy."

"How's that?" Rock asked.

"The joy of the Lord is your strength," Nova said boldly. "It's what helps you go on when things get tough. Whether you're facing a big life challenge, or even if you just lose a shirt."

"My jersey is not just a shirt."

"Joy isn't just happiness either," Nova pressed. "It's what gives us the power to overcome."

Rock shifted his feet. "I know—I need to keep my head in the game. And I don't want to lose my joy."

"Well," Mick said, "you did lose your jersey. Sammy doesn't have it. He never did."

"How do you know that?" Rock demanded.

How does Mick know Sammy never had Rock's jersey?

What was the clue?

Read the solution to find out!

SOLUTION

"Easy," Mick said. "I know Sammy wasn't wearing your jersey because of the way you saw him."

"I don't get it," Rock said.

"You said you were backing out, right? So, it's my guess that you saw Sammy in one of your car mirrors."

"Yeah, so?"

"So," Nova said, catching on, "number 12 looks like 51 when viewed in the mirror. He wasn't wearing your jersey—he was wearing his own!"

"Oh, man!" Rock cried. He turned to Sammy. "They're right! I'm sorry, man! No hard feelings?"

Sammy smiled. "No hard feelings. Just keep your joy, Rock. We'll find your jersey. And we will win this game!"

Word Inspector

". . . the joy of the Lord is your strength."
Nehemiah 8:10

Joy Ride

Help Rock drive to his jersey at the end of the maze!

THE INDESTRUCTIBLE EGG

"I can't help solve any mysteries today after school," Nova said to Mick, standing beside him at the bus stop. "I'm just way too stressed."

Mick scratched his chin. "Been eating too much sugary cereal?"

"No," Nova said with a playful smile on her face. "Too many eggs."

"Eggs?" Mick cried. "Since when do eggs make you stressed?"

Nova turned around and carefully pulled an egg out of her backpack pocket. The egg had two eyes and a mouth drawn on its shell with marker. Nova had even added a cute, tiny bow tie just below its eggshell chin.

"Um . . . I'm not sure if I think that's cute or scary," Mick said.

"It's scary," Nova replied without missing a beat. "This is our newest project in biology class. We've each been given an egg to care for all week long—carrying it everywhere we go. Most importantly, I can't let it break."

"I don't get it," Mick said.

"Basically, it's supposed to show us how hard it is to take care of babies and how hard it is for animals in nature. And you know what? It is incredibly tough. I don't know how anyone does it."

Mick leaned in toward the egg. "Is that a crack?"

Nova rolled her eyes. "Yes. Eggy already has two of them. Almost everyone's egg does. It doesn't take much to get a crack. This one is from when I set him on the breakfast table this morning. Guess I don't know my own strength."

"What happens if Eggy breaks?"

"Then, so does my grade."

"Ouch."

"Tell me about it."

As they waited for the bus, another student, Marvin, showed up and stood near them at the bus stop. Nova introduced Eggy to Marvin, who introduced his egg, Yoke, to Nova. Yoke had marker-smudged blue eyes, a button nose, and three large cracks. Nova considered saying something about the cracks but decided not to.

The three friends made small talk until the bus arrived. Carefully, they entered the bus and took seats beside one another.

"Isn't this hard?" Nova asked Marvin as the bus lurched forward.

"Nah, I'm really not worried," Marvin said.

Mick added, "You don't have to be worried either, Nova. Remember that God's peace can help you during even the toughest of times. You don't have to be troubled. He'll take care of you."

Nova nodded. "I know that's true. It's just difficult when your grade is on the line."

"God knows all about grades," Mick said. "And He knows all about taking care of us. He's going to make sure that even when the enemy tries to crack us, he has no chance of breaking us."

"Yeah!" Marvin shouted, "my point exactly! Yoke is tough as steel."

"I suppose Eggy is, too," Nova said, sounding unsure.

Suddenly, a dog darted across the road and the bus driver slammed on the brakes. The students jarred forward and both Nova and Marvin's eggs shot out of their hands. Nova screamed. Mick jumped forward and grabbed Eggy in mid flight, just before it hit the floor. Marvin's egg, Yoke, wasn't so lucky. It shot out of catching range and smashed against the floor—but didn't break. Then, it rolled down the aisle and hit the bus driver's boot. Marvin jumped up and ran to Yoke. He picked him up and dusted him off. The egg was severely cracked in two more places but not a drop of egg white seeped out.

"That's amazing!" Nova shouted. "Yoke didn't break!"

"It's not so amazing," Mick said. "Marvin knew it wouldn't break."

"What?" said Nova. "How?"

How did Mick know Marvin's egg wouldn't break?

What was the clue?

Read the solution on page 18 to find out!

Mick grabbed Marvin's indestructible egg and knocked on it. "It's hard-boiled," Mick said. "Look at Yoke's eyes and you'll see that the marker ran—from being in hot water, most likely. That's why it cracked just fine—but didn't break."

"Hard-boiled?" Nova shouted. "You can't hard-boil your egg!"

Marvin looked at the bus floor. "I know . . . but that was the only way I thought I could keep it safe."

"Next time," Nova said, "you need to keep it safe yourself. Just like God does. He always has us in His hands."

"The yoke's on you," Mick quipped.

"Ha-ha," Nova replied. "You really crack me up."

Under Investigation

Why is Jesus called the "Prince of Peace"?

What does the phrase to have "peace in the storm" mean?

What is a way you can create peace in your home this week?

Peace Pieces

Redraw the pictures in the correct order in the boxes below to see Eggy and Yoke!

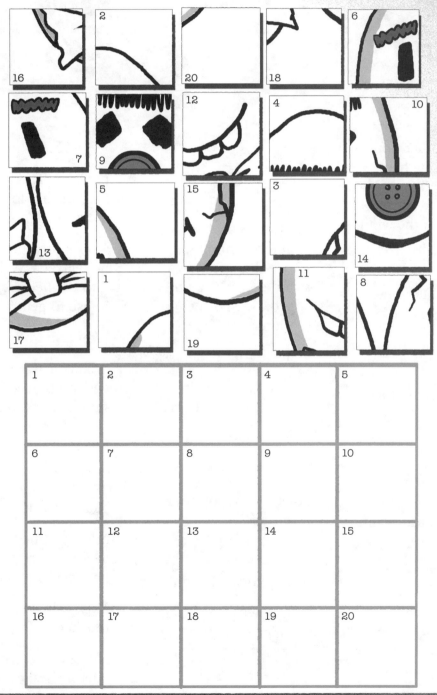

POISON IVY PANIC

Nova was in her front yard washing her bicycle when suddenly Mick came running by, his black hair whipping in the wind.

"Aaaarrrrhhhh!!!" And then, he disappeared around the corner of her house.

Nova twisted her lip, "Mick?" she called.

A moment later, her friend and fellow detective came running around the other side of her house.

"Aaaarrrrhhhh!!!" Then, he disappeared around the corner of her house again.

Nova put down her sponge and turned off the water. A moment later, Mick appeared again, running around the other side of the house. He was making circles.

"Aaaarrrrhhhh!!!"

This time as he passed, Nova threw out her hands and grabbed him by the arm. He dragged her forward several feet, then stopped. "Let go! Let go!" he shouted.

"What's wrong?" she asked.

"I've been poisoned! Viciously poisoned!"

Nova asked, "By whom?"

"By myself!" Nick answered.

"If I let go, do you promise not to run?"

"Maybe!"

Nova let go. Mick didn't run.

"Calm down," Nova said. "Be patient. Remember, God has strengthened you and given you great patience. The Bible says so. So you can do it. Now tell me what happened."

Mick's breathing slowed as he relaxed. "Well, I went into the field behind my house to get my football."

"You don't play football."

"Which is why my football ended up in the field," Mick said. "I went to get it, and when I grabbed it, my hand touched . . ."

"What?"

"Aaaarrrrhhhh!!!"

Nova grabbed Mick's arm again. "Calm down! Great patience! Remember?"

Mick calmed down. "I touched . . . poison ivy!"

Nova let go. "Yikes!" she cried. "How could you let

me touch you?"

"Calm down!" Mick cried.

"I am calm!"

Mick asked, "Do I need to take a bath in tomato juice now?"

Nova said, "I think you only do that when you get sprayed by a skunk."

Mick started to scratch his arm.

"Did you get your football?" Nova asked him.

"No! The ivy attacked me. I reached down to get it and my hand got caught in the green ivy."

"Are you sure it was poison ivy?" asked Nova.

"Yes—I could feel the poisonous oil slide onto my hands from all four leaves on the end of the ivy. It was gross—like icky syrup! You know that's what causes the itching, right? The oil!"

Nova ran back to the faucet and turned on the water again. The hose spat out water, and she grabbed the end of it. "Stand still!" she ordered. "I'm gonna hose you off!"

"No!" Mick shouted. "If you do and the water's warm, the poison ivy could spread!"

"I don't think you have anything to worry about," Nova said very calmly.

"Why not, Nova?" asked Mick.

Why does Nova say that Mick has nothing to worry about?

What was the clue?

Read the solution to find out!

SOLUTION

"You have nothing to worry about," Nova said, "because you don't have poison ivy!"

"How do you know?" Mick demanded.

"Because you said it had four leaves on the end of a branch, right?"

"Right!"

"So, poison ivy only has leaves in clusters of three . . . you've been poisoned by nothing at all."

Mick stopped scratching. "Are you sure?"

"Well . . . ." Nova said with a pause, "let's be sure by washing the sticky stuff off. Then, let's go get a closer look at that plant for a positive ID."

Under Investigation

Why is it important to have patience in everything you do?

What is something you did recently that required patience?

What is something you'll do this week that may require patience?

... being strengthened with all power according to his glorious might so that you may have great endurance and patience. . . .

Colossians 1:11

Follow the Ivy

Which of these plants is poison ivy?
It will take a lot of patience to follow each line and figure it out for sure!

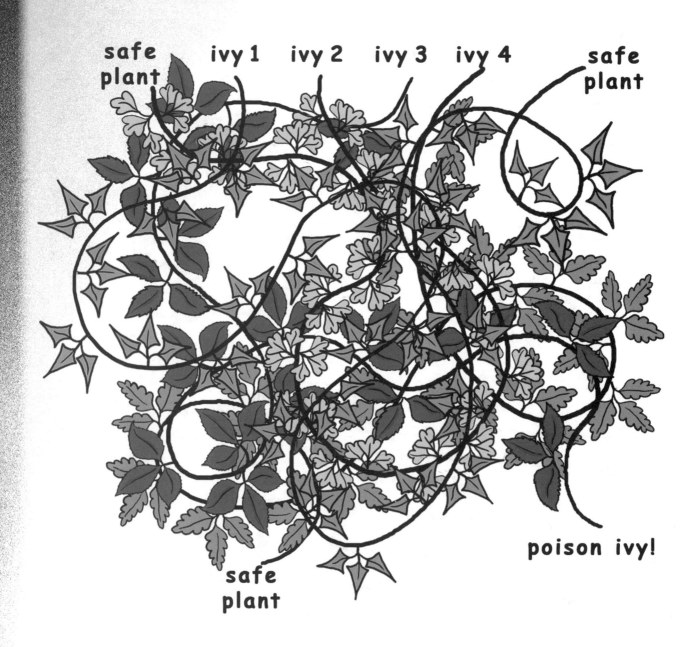

THE SHIN GUARD SWITCH

"**Y**ou're gonna pay for this!"

"I didn't do it!"

Mick and Nova ran up to Rock Johanson, and Mick tapped him on the shoulder. "Hey, Rock, how come every time we run into you, you have someone pinned against a wall?"

"Someone," added Nova, "who's always saying they didn't do it?"

Rock smirked. "It ain't easy being me," he said.

Nova squeezed the bridge of her nose between her finger and thumb. "What happened this time?"

Rock quickly answered, "This time, our team was ready to gear up for soccer and—"

"Hey!" Mick shouted. "You found your jersey!"

He pointed at Rock's red number 51 jersey, proudly hanging on Rock's shoulders with the name "Johanson" on the back.

"Er . . . yeah," Rock said. "It turned out . . . um . . . it was in my gym bag."

Mick glanced at Nova. Nova glanced at Mick.

Mick said, "So, maybe you learned not to jump to conclusions?"

"I don't think so," Nova whispered to her friend.

"I may have been wrong that time," Rock admitted, "but I know I'm not wrong this time. That's why I'm gonna beat up little Billy here."

Billy, the water boy for the Sharks soccer team, was shaking in his shoes. "I didn't do it!" he cried.

"Look," Mick said to Rock. "Nova and I are investigators. We'll be glad to solve this mystery for you. But you have to give us all the facts."

"And you might want to put Billy down," Nova added.

---

23 CD-204035 *Fruit Encounters of the God Kind*

"It's always smarter to be kind to others. There's no use paying back a wrong for a wrong."

Rock continued his firm grip on Billy. "Kind to others, huh?" he exclaimed. "The facts are that after every game, we all give Billy our clothes to wash. He brings them back spick-and-span. Only this time, he decided to be a wise guy."

"What happened?" Mick asked.

Rock let go of Billy. The boy shot him a furrowed brow. Then, he reached down and grabbed a nearby clothes bag. He reached in and pulled out a pair of shin guards—pink shin guards.

"You see that?" Rock shouted. "This wise guy played a practical joke on us and switched our regular shin guards for these pink ones! He expects us to wear these on the field? Ha-ha! Joke's over."

Nova asked Billy, "This isn't a practical joke?"

"Not at all," said Billy.

Mick asked, "Did you ever let these out of your sight?"

"No!" Billy cried. "I washed them late last night at the laundromat. After they dried, my mom put them in this bag, and I hadn't seen them till this morning."

"Oh sure," Rock chided, "you want us to believe your mom

switched our shin guards for pink ones—that she's the jokester?"

Mick asked, "What about today? Anyone have their hands on this bag today?"

Billy thought for a moment. "I don't think so . . . but it's been in the locker room for quite a while. Who knows? Find someone with fifteen pairs of white shin guards, and you'll find the culprit."

"That won't be necessary," Nova said plainly.

"Why not?" asked Rock.

"Because I know who switched the shin guards."

"Who?" asked Billy.

Nova looked at Rock. "You promise to be kind?"

"Yeah."

She looked back at Billy. "You did it," responded Nova. "It's quite clear."

How did Nova know that Billy was responsible for the pink shin guards?

What was the clue?

Read the solution on page 25 to find out!

SOLUTION

"But, I really didn't do it!" Billy cried once more.

"You may not realize it," Nova replied, "but you did. It happened when you washed them. You put in the red jerseys with the white shin guards, didn't you?"

"Yeah, so? It was late," Billy said. "I was running out of time."

"Well, I'm betting you used hot water—and hot water mixed with bright red jerseys will make the color run . . . right into the white shin guards."

Rock's mouth dropped. "Oh, you two are good."

"Thank you," Mick said. "Unfortunately for you, the white shin guards are gone forever. So, it's pink shin guards for all the Sharks."

Rock turned to shout something at Billy, but the water boy had wisely run off.

Under Investigation

How do you feel when someone is kind to you?

When is it especially hard to be kind to someone?

Who is someone you know that you can show kindness to this week?

Crime Stoppers

Who can solve any crime at any time? Find out by completing this color-by-number!
Be sure to use the same color for each numbered shape.

THE CHOCOLATE-FACED BABY

"You do it!" Mick whispered in a hushed voice.

"No, you do it!" Nova whispered back.

"We'll both do it," Mick finally said.

Mick stepped forward and knocked on the large, wooden door. After a few moments, a teenage girl with a smiling baby in her arms and a three-year-old at her side opened the door. The three-year-old waved, and the baby gave the Super Sleuth Investigators a big, gummy smile and a "Goo!" Mick and Nova smiled back.

The baby was covered in chocolate. Her hands and feet were a sticky mess, and brown smudge marks were all over her face. Still, she was as cute as a button.

Mick said, "My name's Mick, and this is Nova. We're the Super Sleuth Investigators. We came as fast as we could. How may we help you?"

The teenager stepped aside and invited Mick and Nova in. She walked to the kitchen. Above the sink, a wide-open window without a screen let in a refreshing breeze.

"This is where it happened," the baby-sitter said, showing them the kitchen. "The thing is, I can't figure out how."

"Well, solving mysteries is what we do," Mick said. "Tell her, Nova."

Nova paused. "Do I have to?"

After Mick shot her a disapproving glance, Nova said dispassionately, "We can solve any crime, any time."

The teenager said, "Well, let me tell you what happened. I came over here at five to sit for Christen and the baby.

Christen is the three-year-old."

Christen waved at Mick and Nova again.

"So, I ran upstairs to get a diaper when suddenly Christen comes running in, shouting. She says to me that the baby has eaten a candy bar!"

Nova smiled. "Someone was hungry."

"No doubt. So I ran downstairs, and there she was, sitting in her playpen, smacking her lips, and licking chocolate off her hands."

The playpen was square, with high sides and net meshing. A torn candy wrapper lay in its center.

"So, what's the problem with that?" Mick asked.

"Well," the baby-sitter said, "not only will the candy

CD-204035 *Fruit Encounters of the God Kind*

spoil her dinner, but what I can't figure out is how she got out of her playpen to get the candy bar! She can crawl, but she can't walk yet!"

Nova looked at Christen. "Did you get your baby sister out of the playpen?" she asked.

Christen shook her head "no" and started crying.

Mick elbowed Nova. "Don't make the child cry," he said.

"Sorry!"

Mick asked, "Where are the candy bars kept?"

The baby-sitter pointed to the floor by the pantry. Sitting there was a small box of candy bars.

"What's this doing on the floor?" Mick asked.

"They're my candy bars," the baby-sitter said. "I brought them over here, and I put them by the back door so I wouldn't forget them when I left."

"Unfortunately," Nova pointed out, "they're low enough for even a crawling baby to reach."

Mick looked at the candy bars. They were peanut bars covered in milk chocolate—his favorite.

"But how'd she get out of the playpen?" the baby-sitter wondered aloud.

Mick looked at Nova. Nova looked at Christen. Christen started crying again.

"C'mon," Mick said, "there's no way that little girl could have picked the baby up and gotten her out of that playpen. That's a tall playpen." Nova nodded, acknowledging that Mick was right.

"She's always been a good baby," the baby-sitter said. "I just don't know what got into her."

"Well, that says a lot," Nova stated. "God is good, and He wants us to follow in His footsteps. That's why He gave us goodness as one of the fruit of the Spirit. Even if we mess up, He knows we're trying to live good lives, giving glory to Him."

"I'm sure she is good," Mick said. "And I think I know exactly how she got to the candy."

The baby-sitter's mouth dropped open. "You do?"

Do you know how the baby got the candy?

What was the clue?

Read the solution on page 29 to find out!

SOLUTION

"Actually," Mick said, "the baby didn't get to the candy at all. The candy got to her. Or, more accurately, some of the candy got to her."

"I don't understand," the baby-sitter said. "You think someone gave her candy?"

"I do," Nova said. "Most likely Christen."

"But why would Christen give the baby candy to eat?"

"She didn't," Mick stated. "The baby couldn't eat the candy even if she had wanted to. The first thing I noticed when I came in was that she has no teeth—but the candy bars are filled with peanuts!"

Looking at Christen, Nova said, "Someone must have eaten some of the candy before dinner time . . . and to get off the hook, she framed the baby . . . by placing a wrapper in her playpen and smearing chocolate all over her face."

"Is that right, Christen?" the baby-sitter asked. Christen's eyes watered up again. The baby-sitter said, "Open your mouth!" When Christen did, there were peanut remains between her teeth.

"Mystery solved!" Mick said. "Now, more importantly, can I have one of the bars as a souvenir?"

Under Investigation

Why does God say it is important to live a good life?

Where does goodness come from? (Look up Psalm 100:5 for a hint!)

What is a good thing you can do this week that will give glory to God?

Live such good lives that [others] will see the
good things you do and will give glory to God. . . .
1 Peter 2:12 NCV

Code Breaker!

How can you stop evil in its tracks?
Crack the chocolate bar code below to find out!

‾4‾ ‾15‾ ‾14‾ ‾15‾ ‾20‾ ‾2‾ ‾5‾ ‾15‾ ‾22‾ ‾5‾ ‾18‾ ‾3‾ ‾15‾ ‾13‾ ‾5‾

‾2‾ ‾25‾ ‾5‾ ‾22‾ ‾9‾ ‾12‾' ‾2‾ ‾21‾ ‾20‾ ‾15‾ ‾22‾ ‾5‾ ‾18‾ ‾3‾ ‾15‾ ‾13‾ ‾5‾

‾5‾ ‾22‾ ‾9‾ ‾12‾ ‾23‾ ‾9‾ ‾20‾ ‾8‾ ‾7‾ ‾15‾ ‾15‾ ‾4‾. Romans 12:21

| A 1 | B 2 | C 3 | D 4 | E 5 | F 6 | G 7 | H 8 | I 9 | J 10 | K 11 | L 12 | M 13 |
| N 14 | O 15 | P 16 | Q 17 | R 18 | S 19 | T 20 | U 21 | V 22 | W 23 | X 24 | Y 25 | Z 26 |

THE SPLASHED PRINCIPAL

"We are so in trouble!" Milly said to Mick and Nova.

"That's why we're here," Mick said. "You've called in the best."

Nova looked surprised, "You mean us?"

Mick gently shoved her aside. He said to Milly, "Now, what seems to be the problem?"

Milly and her two friends Nilly and Willy were standing by a shiny car with buckets and sponges at their feet. A short distance away stood a large gas station with five pumps and a big "Car Wash" sign.

Milly pointed to the gas station. "Our school principal, Mr. Walker, is in there!" she said. "He's in the rest room getting dry."

Mick's face crinkled. "Dry? Why was he wet?"

Milly looked at the ground. She pointed to three hoses that were leaking water. "One of us squirted him. But none of us thinks it was us."

"Well, if he's wet," Nova said, "then someone must have done it."

"Exactly," said Milly. "That's why we brought you here. We need to figure out who did it, so we don't accidentally do it again.

It kinda cuts down on car wash sales when customers get soaked."

"I can see how that would be a damper," Mick punned.

Nova shook her head at Mick and asked, "Did you each have a hose?"

Milly nodded. "And they were all on full blast, so we could finish faster. Plus, we each had a bucket and a sponge. The thing is, none of us thinks we had our hoses pointed at him. Mine was pointed at the tires—I was cleaning them off. Nilly was washing the hood of his car, so her hose was aiming there. And Willy was using his sponge on the back license plate. He had his hose pointed up between scrubs."

Mick asked, "Where was Mr. Walker standing?"

"He was behind the three of us."

"Behind you?"

"Yes, watching."

Mick scratched his chin. "And the three of you were facing the car."

"Exactly," said Milly. "It makes no sense."

Nova walked to the side of the car and rubbed a small spot on the driver's window with her fingers.

"What are you thinking?" Mick asked.

Nova said, "Is it possible the water from someone's hose bounced off the car and sprayed back? Milly said they were on full blast."

Mick looked at Milly, Nilly, and Willy. All three were dry, except their hands and knees. "I don't think so," he said. "If that were the case, at least one of these guys would be wet, too."

The Super Sleuth Investigators scratched their heads until they saw a figure approaching. They recognized the soggy man to be Mr. Walker. His expression was flat as he slowly walked toward them. In his hand, was a paper towel, which he dabbed on the top of his head. His brown toupee looked like it was about to slide off.

Mick held out his hand for a handshake. Mr. Walker smiled. "So," he said, "I hear you and Nova are sort of private eyes."

"No 'sort of' about it,"

Mick said proudly. "Solving mysteries is what we do."

"So, do you know who sprayed me with water?" Mr. Walker asked. "Because they don't seem to know."

"Absolutely!" Mick responded.

"You do?" Milly shouted.

"God has given me the fruit of faithfulness," Mick said. "I've learned that by being faithful and sticking with it, the answer to about every mystery will soon come."

"So, what is the answer?" Mr. Walker asked.

Do you know who sprayed Mr. Walker with water?

What was the clue?

Read the solution to find out!

SOLUTION

"The answer is quite simple," Mick said. "The biggest clue was when I saw you approach, wiping the top of your head. I had just assumed you got sprayed in the face, but it looks to me like you got sprayed on top of your head."

"Exactly," said Mr. Walker. "But, what does that prove?"

"That proves," Nova said, "that the water must have come from above."

"Right!" said Nick. "And the only way water can come down is if it goes up in the first place. And the only one of these three with a water hose pointed up, at full power, was Willy."

"What goes up must come down," Nova said.

"Good job!" Milly shouted.

Willy didn't waste a moment to apologize and Mr. Walker accepted. "I know God will use you to do great things at this car wash," he said, "as you stay faithful and keep those hoses pointed away from me!"

Under Investigation

What does it mean to be faithful in doing a task?

What does it mean when friends are faithful to each other?

How will you demonstrate faithfulness this week?

Dot-to-Dot

Complete this dot-to-dot drawing to see what Mick and Nova are washing.

THE PLANE THAT TOOK A NOSEDIVE

Mick and Nova biked to the spot where the caller said they needed to be. When they got there, they saw nothing but a large field with weeds growing everywhere and a few small shrubs. Houses stood in the distance.

"You sure this is the place?" Nova asked.

Mick hopped off his bicycle. Bubble gum wrappers lay on the ground, and some were stuck on a bush. A few twigs had been broken, and the grass had recently been stepped on. Mick stood up again and shaded his eyes with his hand. He scouted the area beyond the field. "There!" he said. In the distance, he saw a boy at one of the houses waving his hands at them.

The two investigators hopped back on their bikes and took off toward the house. When they got there, they saw a teenage boy chewing gum and holding a broken remote-controlled

plane in his hands. One of the wings was completely broken off from the body.

A man stood over him with his hands on his hips.

After Mick and Nova put their bikes down, Mick said to the teenager, "You must be Nathan. We thought we were supposed to meet you down in the field."

The boy nodded. "You must be the investigators. Well, I wasn't going to leave my plane a couple of hundred feet away while I waited for you. And, quite honestly, I was hoping for someone . . . taller."

"Height doesn't matter," Nova said. "It's smarts that count."

"What seems to be the problem?" Mick asked.

Suddenly the man spoke up. "The problem is, this kid's loud plane crashed right into my yard! Look at that gash in my lawn!"

"It didn't crash!" Nathan shouted. "I think he shot it down!"

"Whoa," Nova said. "A gentle answer turns away wrath, guys—the Bible says so in Proverbs 15:1. So let's be cool and gentle about this. I'm sure no one meant to ruin the plane or the yard."

"Do you know what this is?" Nathan asked. "It's a CTX 4000—a very expensive remote-controlled plane. Dual motors, 60-yard radius, quantum airlift. I had just buffed the underside. It was perfect. Now it's ruined!"

"I understand you're upset,"

Mick said, "but shouting isn't going to help us solve the mystery about why it crashed."

The man added, "And gashed my property."

"And gashed your property," Mick allowed.

Mick pointed to a tree about 20 feet away. "Is it possible the tree caused interference with your remote control signal?"

Nathan seemed to have lost interest. "No," he said flatly. "It has a 900-quam megahertz signal that can penetrate through walls. A tree isn't going to cause any troubles."

"Not even if the leaves might disorient the signal?" Nova offered.

Nathan shook his head.

The man pointed to an electrical wire stemming from his roof to a tall pole. "Do you think it may have caught on the wire and was knocked down?"

Nathan said, "No, I saw it very clearly. It was flying straight, coming around for a turn, when suddenly it went into a nosedive. It didn't run into anything."

"Except my lawn," the man noted.

"Except your lawn," Nova said.

Nathan pulled the battery out of the bottom of the plane and blew on it. He held it up to the sunlight. "It's still at 75 percent. No problem there."

Mick asked, "How about the battery in your remote control transmitter?"

Nova interrupted, "Nope, it wasn't that. But I know exactly what it was."

"You do?" Mick, Nathan, and the man said at once.

"I do!" Nova responded.

Do you know what caused the plane to take a nosedive?

What was the clue?

Read the solution to find out!

SOLUTION

"The answer to this one is mathematical," Nova stated. "You said this fancy remote-controlled plane can fly up to 60 yards away from you, correct?"

Nathan nodded. "Yeah. It's a CTX 4000."

"I see where you're going with this," Mick said. "Nathan, you yourself said that this house was a couple of hundred feet from where you were standing—which is where we were when we first arrived. We saw your gum wrappers."

"So?" Nathan asked.

"So," explained Nova, "there are three feet in a yard. So that means your plane can only fly 180 feet away from you. It was clearly at least 20 feet outside of remote-controlled range."

"And thus the nosedive," said Mick.

"I guess it was my fault then. I'm sorry," Nathan said to the man gently.

"No problem," the man finally smiled. I may have overreacted. It's just grass. Why don't you help me fill in the worst parts?"

Under Investigation

What does it mean to be gentle?

Is being gentle the same as being weak?

What is something you will do this week to exercise your gentleness?

Just Plane Different

Being gentle makes you strong inside—changing you from the inside out!
Speaking of changes, can you see the 10 differences between these two pictures?

THE CUPCAKE CULPRIT

"Happy birthday, Willy!"

Mick and Nova joined Milly and Nilly for Willy's twelfth birthday party. Milly said inviting them was the least they could do. Mick and Nova had saved them all from Mr. Walker's wrath after they had soaked him at their car wash.

When Mick and Nova arrived, Milly gave each of them a hug. Nilly gave them a sweaty, sticky high five (she'd been playing ball with Willy earlier), and Willy waved from the other side of the yard. After playing around in the backyard, the five kids went inside.

"Tell us about some of the crimes you've solved!" Milly said.

Nova said, "We don't want to bore you."

Mick disagreed, "Our adventures are anything but boring!"

When it came time to open presents, Willy sat down with everyone and opened each one. Milly gave him a SuperCoolMan action figure. Nilly gave him a Street Raider XIV video game.

Mick and Nova gave him a fingerprint kit. He seemed to like the video game the most. Nilly tried taking fingerprints of the action figure, but all she did was get ink smudges on his plastic hands.

When it was time for birthday sweets, Willy's mother entered the room to say hello to everyone.

She returned to the kitchen. Suddenly, the five kids heard a gasp. They ran to her.

"What's wrong?" Mick asked Willy's mother.

She pointed to the cupcakes on the refrigerator shelf. Each one had a hole in its center . . . a hole the size of a finger.

Nova pushed her way to the front of the crowd around the refrigerator. "Someone poked holes in the cupcakes?" she asked.

"They got right to the creamy filling," said Willy's mother.

"Apparently," said Mick, "someone didn't have the self-control to wait and eat them with the rest of us."

"God gave us self-control," said Nova. "He wants us to be disciplined so we can control ourselves and be good examples to others."

"Well, someone wasn't being a great example today," said

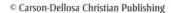

Mick. "Who else is in the house?"

Willy's mother said, "It's just us—me and the five of you."

"That means one of us did it," said Mick. "The question is, who?"

Everyone looked at each other.

"Well, you can count me out," said Willy's mother. "When I put these cupcakes in here, they were fine. I haven't seen them since."

"No, it couldn't have been you," said Mick. "The holes are a bit small for your fingers."

"Not that you have big fingers," Nova said, her face turning red. "It's just that we have small ones."

Everyone held up their fingers and compared them. Any one of them could have fit in the holes.

Mick looked at each person's mouth, hoping to see some cupcake crumbs. Milly had some kind of gloss on her lips. Nilly's lips just looked normal. Willy's were wet from drinking a soft drink, but there was no evidence of cupcake remains.

"I guess we'll never know who did it," said Milly. "Unless someone fesses up."

"Or, unless I tell you," said Mick.

"You know who did this?" Willy's mother asked.

Mick nodded. "They don't call me a 'super' sleuth investigator for nothing."

Do you know who sampled the cupcakes?

What was the clue?

Read the solution to find out!

SOLUTION

"The person who put a finger in these cupcakes is the one whose fingers were sticky when we first arrived. I thought it was from playing ball . . . but I'm betting it was from sugar."

All eyes turned and looked at Nilly. She blushed.

"Just couldn't help yourself, huh?" Nova asked.

Nilly shook her head.

"I guess Nilly needs a good dose of self-control," said Willy's mother. Then, she turned around and opened the oven. "The good news is, I have a second batch that's just about done!"

Everyone cheered. She handed the tray of finger-poked cupcakes to Nilly. "These are yours," she said. "We'll take the fresh ones!"

Under Investigation

What is self-control?

How can you do things better if you use self-control?

What is something you'll do this week that will require self-control?

For God did not give us a spirit of timidity, but a spirit of power, of love and of self-discipline.

2 Timothy 1:7

Count 'em!

There are a bunch of cupcakes on this page! Can you count them all?

_____ cupcakes

CD-204035 *Fruit Encounters of the God Kind*

THE DISAPPEARING MINNOWS

"The frogs ate my fish!" exclaimed Penny as she led Mick and Nova down to her family's pond. Penny lived on a large farm with all sorts of interesting animals, from horses to ostriches.

"This is a beautiful farm," said Nova as she spied two cats tussling in the grass.

"Yeah," Penny said, "until the animals start eating each other."

Nova shot Mick a sideways glance. He returned it.

When the three reached the pond, Nova didn't see much of anything, except a few birds playing in the water at the far end. The tall grass at the edge of the water bent underneath her feet, and the dirt turned to mud. She looked into the murky water and shook her head. "I'm not sure what you want us to look for," she said.

Penny huffed.

Mick said, "We're investigators, Penny. I'm sure you hired us to solve a mystery. But what is it?"

"The mystery," Penny said, "is what happened to my fish? I came out here a couple of weeks ago, and there were a bunch of small fish in the pond. I named them all—from A to Z."

"You counted 26 fish?" Mick asked.

"And kept track of who was who?" Nova asked.

"Well," Penny admitted, "keeping track of them wasn't as easy as naming them. But that doesn't matter. What I want to know is, what happened to them?"

Mick asked, "What did they look like?"

They were so cute!" Penny said. "Little ones, like minnows. Just babies. I was looking forward to all of them growing up, so that I could go fishing and catch them and rename them and throw them back in the pond."

"Maybe they're just in the middle of the pond where we can't see," Mick said.

Penny pointed to a small canoe on the far bank of the pond. "I went out to the middle. Nothing."

Nova pushed aside more blades of grass and leaned down. A small frog jumped at her. "Augh!" she cried, jumping back herself. Suddenly three more tiny frogs jumped out at her. Nova stepped backward quickly and suppressed another scream. "Gross!"

CD-204035 *Fruit Encounters of the God Kind*

Penny rolled her eyes. "I know it. They're everywhere. And I think they ate my minnows. That's what I want to know. Did they do it? Or, did another animal? Whoever ate my minnows has to go."

Nova bit her lower lip. "Um . . . how can we tell that?"

"I think you should dissect one," said Penny.

"Gross! Nuh-uh! That's where I draw the line!" Nova said.

"Yeah," Mick said to Penny, "we don't normally dissect animals to solve mysteries."

Nova looked relieved.

Penny kicked the grass with her foot and threw her fist through the air. "This makes me so mad!" she cried. "Who ate my minnows?"

"Don't get upset," Nova said to Penny. "Remember, God has given you the fruit of self-control."

Penny huffed again. "I know. I just don't like not knowing!"

"Well, God has given you the fruit of patience, too," Mick said. "In fact, He's given you lots of fruit— love, joy, peace, patience, kindness, goodness, faithfulness, gentleness, and self-control. They all work together to help you be the person God has called you to be!"

"Putting them together makes a BIG difference," Nova admitted. "And putting all of the clues in this mystery together makes a big difference, too."

"You know what ate my minnows?" Penny asked.

"I do," Nova said.

SOLUTION

"Well, you never said they were minnows for sure. You just said they looked like them," Nova stated.

"Yes," Mick said, "so what were they then?"

"Since there are frogs everywhere, I'm betting they were baby frogs—tadpoles! As tadpoles, they had no feet. They look like fish, but then, they sprout feet and lose their tails, and can come onto land."

"Which is why you can't find any 'minnows' anymore," said Mick. "Good deduction, Nova!"

"Hey," she said, "the best solutions come when you put all of the pieces together!"

Do you know what happened to Penny's minnows?

What was the clue?

Read the solution to find out!

Under Investigation

Why is it important to have all of the fruit of the Spirit in your life?

What fruit did Jesus demonstrate during His time on Earth?

Which fruit of the Spirit do you think work together best in your life?

But if anyone obeys his word, God's love is truly made complete in him. This is how we know we are in him: Whoever claims to live in him must walk as Jesus did.

1 John 2:5-6

Putting It Together

The fruit of the Spirit all work together like one complete puzzle! Match up the puzzle pieces by coloring each verse's text with its reference using the same color.

THE STINKY SULFUR INCIDENT

As they walked into the large warehouse, Mick and Nova immediately put their hands over their noses.

"Ugh!" Nova cried. "What is that smell?"

"Sulfur," said a man, approaching them. He held out his hand. "I'm Mr. Butler. I'm the one who called."

Mick said, "I'm Mick, and this is Nova. We're with Super Sleuth Investigations. How may we be of service?"

Mr. Butler let out a slow breath. "You smell that?"

Nova actually laughed.

"How can you not?" The smell was piercing.

"It does smell like sulfur," Mick said. "You know sulfur is a poisonous gas, don't you?"

Mr. Butler nodded. "Well, nothing is dying around here. It just smells like it. We've even caught a rodent or two, so I'm sure it's safe. Listen, here's the reason I'm hiring you: we need to track down what's causing this smell. This warehouse used to belong to a box manufacturer. You know, cardboard boxes? Well, they closed down, and I bought the warehouse to start my

own business. But I won't be able to get anyone to work here because of the smell."

"That's the truth," Nova said. "So we need to track down what's causing the smell?"

"Exactly. And the quicker, the better. I think it's getting into my clothing."

Mick smiled. "Shouldn't be a problem. Show us around."

Mr. Butler led the way. They walked through an area of cubicles first. Only a few items remained here and there. It looked as though it was once a bustling office: a stapler, a political cartoon about gasoline prices, a wall calendar turned to April, a wastebasket with a half-eaten chocolate bar inside. Other than that, it was completely empty.

They turned the corner and walked through some hanging plastic. The smell became stronger. As far in front of them as they could see, were row after row of steel shelves. Many were bare, but some contained open boxes, closed boxes, flat boxes—just boxes, boxes, and more boxes. They stayed silent for a moment and heard a rodent or two running around. Nova shivered.

"Anyway," said Mr. Butler, "this is the main warehouse. Bet you can't guess what they did in here? That's right! As I told you, they made boxes."

Mick's foot hit a piece of candy lying on the floor. It shot across the room. "Sorry," he said.

Mr. Butler chuckled. "What, you think you're gonna mess this place up? Naw, I'm gonna gut it. Got boxes everywhere . . . and an occasional piece of candy. It's kind of sad. This was a real family-oriented workplace. Right before they shut down, they had a holiday party here for the workers and their families. Guess they weren't too happy to find out the next week that they didn't have jobs."

"You think someone was vindictive?" asked Nova. "Maybe hid a block of sulfur somewhere?"

"Actually," Mick said, "sulfur is odorless. It only stinks when it burns and the gas is released."

"How do you know that?" Nova asked with a smile.

"Earth science."

"So how are you kids gonna solve this one?" asked Mr. Butler. "You need anything from me?"

Mick said, "Well, we've got the fruit of the Spirit in our lives. With God's love, joy, peace, patience, kindness, goodness, faithfulness, gentleness, and self-control, we can conquer anything!"

Nova smiled wide. "Even tough mysteries."

"Ah, this one isn't that tough," said Mick. "Actually it's quite easy."

"Don't tell me you know what's causing that smell already!" said Mr. Butler.

"Of course I do," said Mick.

Do you know what's causing the sulfur smell?

What was the clue?

Read the solution on page 46 to find out!

SOLUTION

"My first clue," said Mick, "was when you said they celebrated a holiday event for families here. I wondered what holiday that could be."

"The calendar!" said Nova. "It was set to April!"

"And Easter is always in late March or early April," Mick said. "So then, I deduced that the Easter celebration might have included an egg hunt."

"And that makes perfect sense!" said Mr. Butler, "because when eggs go rotten, they smell like—"

All three said, "Sulfur."

"So, we just need to do an egg hunt of our own?" asked Mr. Butler.

"I think so," said Mick. "Find the forgotten eggs and you've got your culprit!"

Under Investigation

With the fruit of the Spirit active in your life, how are you different?

How can you make the fruit of the Spirit stronger in your life?

Why do you think God gave you the fruit of the Spirit?

Word Inspector

Super Scramble

Unscramble the fruit of the Spirit.
Then, unscramble the letters in the circles to complete the sentence below!

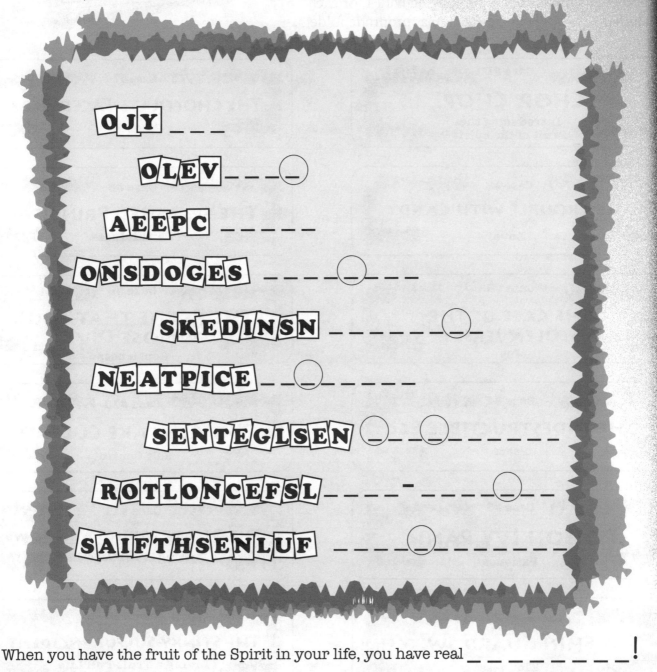

OJY _ _ _

OLEV _ _ _ _ (_)

AEEPC _ _ _ _ _ _

ONSDOGES _ _ _ (_) _ _ _ _

SKEDINSN _ _ _ _ _ _ (_) _

NEATPICE _ (_) _ _ _ _ _ _

SENTEGLSEN (_) _ _ _ _ (_) _ _ _ _

ROTLONCEFSL _ _ _ _ - _ _ _ (_) _ _

SAIFTHSENLUF _ _ _ _ (_) _ _ _ _ _ _

When you have the fruit of the Spirit in your life, you have real _ _ _ _ _ _ _ _ _ _!

SUPER SLEUTH CASE FILES

Create case files for your own Super Sleuths to solve during free class time. Make 12 copies of page one of this book, trim the margins, and attach each to the cover of a file folder. Copy the labels below onto extra large ($^{15}/_{16}$" x 3 $^{7}/_{16}$", 2.38 cm x 8.73 cm) file folder labels or simply cut them out and tape them to the file folder tabs. Copy each mystery story once and copy enough corresponding activities for each student. Then, place them in the appropriate folders.

Case #1

CHOP, CHOP!

Introducing the Fruit of the Spirit

Case #2

THE TROUBLE WITH CANDY

Love

Case #3

THE CASE OF THE STOLEN JERSEY

Joy

Case #4

THE INDESTRUCTIBLE EGG

Peace

Case #5

POISON IVY PANIC

Patience

Case #6

THE SHIN GUARD SWITCH

Kindness

Case #7

THE CHOCOLATE-FACED BABY

Goodness

Case #8

THE SPLASHED PRINCIPAL

Faithfulness

Case #9

THE PLANE THAT TOOK A NOSE DIVE

Gentleness

Case #10

THE CUPCAKE CULPRIT

Self-Control

Case #11

THE DISAPPEARING MINNOWS

Putting It All Together

Case #12

THE STINKY SULFUR INCIDENT

Living a Fruit-Full Life